Why You Don't Need A Divorce Attorney

One Paralegal's Take On Divorce,
Responsibility And Compromise

By Tim Blankenship

CONTENTS

ACKNOWLEDGMENTS

I have to hand it to my wife, Elia. She supports every single endeavor I take on and encourages me to do others I wouldn't do on my own. I wouldn't be where I am today in life professionally or personally and would not attempt half the things I have accomplished over the years without her. You are the engine that keeps me going. Woman, I love you!

INTRODUCTION

My name is Tim Blankenship and I own a Legal Document Assistant Company in Los Angeles, California called Divorce661 and can be found at www.divorce661.com. We provide an affordable approach to getting divorced in California providing both a full service solution and a do-it-yourself divorce solution at www.CaliforniaDivorceTutor.com. I wrote this book to show you that there is a better way of getting divorced than going the route of hiring a divorce attorney. Thank you for reading this book. I think you will enjoy it and find it very interesting and useful whether you are thinking about divorce, in the middle of a divorce, or know someone who is going through divorce.

Here's My Story

Everybody has their story of where they are and how they ended up there. Well, here's mine. It is nothing very exciting, but more interesting than anything else. How did I go from high school, to the Marine Corps during Desert Storm to becoming a Police Officer for the Los Angeles Police Department and then end up helping people with their divorce?

All I can say is that "Life Happened".

After I got out of the Marine Corps I ended up working as a Police Officer for what was then the Metropolitan Transportation Authority Police Department. Back in 1994 I had applied for several law enforcement agencies and the MTA Police Department hired me first. A few years later, our agency was merged into the Los Angeles Police Department where I worked until 2007.

My life up through this point was great. I was married, had two children, a house, a great job and things were going well. Then it happened. In 2006 I had began selling real estate on the side as there was great money to be made due to the housing boom. I had sold real estate with my wife for about a year and we were making money hand over fist. So much so, that I decided to quit my job with LAPD to focus full time on real estate. At this point my wife and I had our own real estate team as well as working with investors flipping homes so making the move made sense.

Oh boy did we think we were so smart and set for life. But we already know how this turns out, right? There are so many stories and so many people that lost everything when the real estate market and the economy collapsed. And we were no exception. It was gone as fast as it came.

Scrambling to figure out a way to make money, I worked as a Private Investigator for a while and was trying to decide what to do with my life. I had started back at school to finish my degree and it was at that point I decided I wanted to go to law school and become a lawyer.

So I did. Well, I started going to law school anyways. Let me give you a glimpse of my life at this point. I was going to law school, started volunteering at the Los Angeles Counties Court self help centers, volunteered as an intern for the Los Angeles Superior Court System which finally led to a full time job as a paralegal working for a law firm. I was 41 years old and have a wife and two children to support and just never thought I would be where I was at that point in my life. But I just kept plugging away.

While working for a law firm that handles divorce and while still attending law school, I slowly became dismayed at what attorneys actually do. Especially as it relates to divorce. I saw families further torn apart, perhaps worse than if they had not had attorneys. I saw people spend 10's of thousands of dollars on fighting their spouse throughout the divorce process. I saw attorneys giving advice that in no way shape or form was in their clients or their families best interest.

And again I was at a crossroads of what I should really be doing. So I started doing a little research with the belief that there had to be a better way to get through this thing we call divorce. I discovered that there was a not very well known way of helping people with their divorce without having to go to law school and without having to become a lawyer. I also learned that there was no one in my local area providing these services.

What I am referring to is what is known as a Legal Document Assistant. And it just happened to turn out that because I had my degree and had worked for the courts and a law firm that I already met the requirements to become registered to provide these services. So I got registered as a Legal Document Assistant, continued to work as a paralegal for the law firm and was still attending law school.

I started slowly in the evenings, after work and when not studying for law school to start marketing my business as a Legal Document Assistant. Fortunately, I had honed my skills at marketing which I learned in my short stint with real estate, especially online, so I knew I had a pretty good chance of getting my business off the ground. Slowly but surely I started picking up clients. I would meet them at their home or at Starbucks. I was just starting out, so did not have an office and really didn't know how well this business venture might turn out.

It had been maybe 2 months since I started helping people part time with their divorce with my Legal Document Assistant business. One day at work, I get called into the partner attorney's office and he tells me that he has to let me go. I was being fired? It turns out he found out that I had started a business and said that it was a conflict of interest. I guarantee that had I worked at any other law firm that this would not have happened. This was just the nature of this particular law firm.

It was September, 2012 and I found myself realizing at that moment that my little part time business just became a full time business that absolutely had to work out. This was no longer just an extra income experiment, it was now my primary way of earning money. So I got to work doing what I know how to do best. That is marketing.

Fast forward to 2016 and I am still here - And in a big way. I have been able to take a little part time business and turn it into a rapidly expanding full service Legal Document Assistant company in California handling approximately 30+ divorce cases per month. I have published over 1,200 articles online, recorded over 1000 videos and have a podcast that I broadcast daily on. I have helped clients going through divorce save 100's of thousands of dollars in attorney fees over the years. I am still here, but life sure has its challenges.

About This Book

So why write a book? With all the content that I have produced over the years, I still get the same questions over and over every day. I wanted to put all the content I have produced, whether written or spoken into a single format for people to be able to find the information they need. In addition, I wanted to inform the public about what Legal Documents Assistants really are and what we can really do so people understand that there are better ways to go through divorce than to hire an attorney.

This book will be broken down into chapters which will have questions that I have been asked over the years with the answers that I have given over and over again. And this won't be just a question and answer session, I will also be giving you my perspective and personal opinion along the way on how I feel about certain situations related to divorce based upon my experience in having helped 1000's of people with their divorce.

I hope you learn from this book, not only from my experience in helping people with their divorce, but to fully understand that there is a better way to get through your divorce rather than hiring an attorney.

This book is written with the intention of getting spouses to sit down and figure out how they can best get through their divorce. It is to put in your face that it is your responsibility to deal with this as an adult and not let emotion or whatever else get in the way, causing you to throw away money because you are mad at each other. It is to tell you to compromise with each other and if you have children to make decisions in the children's best interest and not yours.

I think it is ridiculous that people fight during divorce. I can't stand the pettiness that is involved, the name calling and irrational behavior that can consume you. Knock it off and act like the adult you are! I know, harsh words, I told you that I would be sharing my perspective. And you might not like it and that's okay.

Now, on this high horse rant of mine, I know that there are folks out there that absolutely need to have an attorney. There are evil doers out there looking to do you harm and you need to protect yourself. This book is not for you and I don't want you to take offense. I am on your side. And to you evil doers who create chaos and harm others... Shame on you.

Chapter 1

DIVORCE - AN EPIDEMIC

Divorce is everywhere, all around us. Our friends are getting divorced, our parents are getting divorced, our children are getting divorced. My children's friends parents all seem to be divorced. My divorce paralegal firm handles approximately 30 divorce cases every month and we are just one company in one town in America. The phone literally rings off the hook each and every day and I keep thinking to myself, "Isn't everyone already divorced yet?" Indeed, good for business, but sad to see so many people going through this. While I wish I had a cure for divorce, I will just have to continue feeling good about providing a divorce solution to people that makes going through divorce a much more comfortable experience.

What Is The Divorce Rate?

There is much debate on this topic. If you were to do a Google search, you would come across numerous articles that say the divorce rate is around the 40% to 50% mark. Honestly, the actual rate at which people are divorcing is not important except to show that it is pretty high. From personal experience, all I can say is that there is a lot of divorce going on. And don't get me started on my opinion on where we are going with the younger generations. So much is changing with our culture. 40 or so years ago people got married young, got a job and worked that one job for 30 years. These days the younger folks are not getting married until well into their 30's and working at multiple jobs. I just wonder if this trend will carry over into relationships. I think it will and already has.

Why People Divorce

Obviously I don't have the answer to why people divorce. In fact, I don't really even want to discuss this topic. You want to know why? Because it just does not matter. I am not saying you don't matter, just that learning the reasons why are not going to help you with what you have going on in your life, except to learn that you are not alone.

We know all the negative things that spouses do that causes divorce, but what about where spouses just grow apart and it is not working anymore? In my business I see more people simply growing apart than anything else. And it may be less about growing apart and more about that they did not continue to grow together as a unit.

I feel that in most cases divorce is not a surprise. What I mean to say is that if the relationship is so poor that one of you feels that it is bad enough to feel it necessary to file for divorce, or even start talking divorce, that the other party has to have some idea that things are not very rosy.

That said, there are some exceptions. I have lots of women clients that say that nothing is really wrong, that things are just the same as always. Or they will say that they don't really know why they are not happy, they are just not happy.

What does this tell us? I don't know, but it could mean that men and women are just different. How profound a statement, right? It may be a reason or It may be an excuse, but it seems some men feel that to go to work, provide shelter, food and safety is enough. But I think we need to get out of that caveman style mentality if we want to see any reversal of the divorce epidemic.

But we are not here to talk about the why. We are here to talk about the how. How are you going to get through this divorce and how are things going to look on the other end of this? I will tell you, based upon my clients conversations and experiences, that there is light at the end of the tunnel. That as bad as it might seem while you are going through divorce, that happiness will reenter your life soon after.

Women Lead In Filing For Divorce

I could research the statistic, but I don't have to. Women take the lead in initiating the divorce process. In my business, most of my inquiries about divorce are from women and in suit, women are the ones to come in to our offices and initiate the divorce process. If I had to put a number to it, I would put it at about 80% of the time. Why is this? In my experience I have found that there is just something about the men who simply stick their head in the sand and don't want to deal with the issues. This is not a blanket statement for all men, but I see this all too often. Even when the women starts the divorce process, we are still having to drag most men through the process. The men are not uncooperative as much as they just don't want to deal with it.

Chapter 2

DIVORCE & FEAR

How & When To Tell Your Spouse
You Want A Divorce

This is going to be different for everyone of course, but I could probably provide you a little help here seeing as I deal with so many people going through divorce. I think the "How" and "When" you tell your spouse can really make a difference on how well your divorce case ultimately plays out.

How are you going to tell your spouse you want a divorce? Remember here that we are talking about folks trying to go through an amicable divorce and we are trying to set up a situation where the environment is best suited for having the conversation. I would suggest that you plan this out so that you are not placed in a situation where you get upset at your spouse and just blurt it out, "I want a divorce!" We want to do this amicably, so even if there is a lot of upset and emotion you can handle this as a business decision so both of you can deal with what's about to happen.

Remember, as I stated previously, (and I am talking to you women right now) that your husband may have absolutely no idea you are about to drop this on him, so the how and the when are going to really matter. Give it some thought and think about how your week normally happens. Think about your schedule, when the kids are home or at practice, etc. Make sure to be in a place that is quiet and that you have ample time to discuss as much as possible and that you don't have to run out for some errand in 10 minutes, interrupting the conversation. You are going to want to get this out in a single conversation.

Not everything will be discussed here of course, but you want to make sure your spouse fully understands that you are not bringing this up as casual conversation, but that this is really happening.

Now for the when. I think I will answer this in two ways. "When" as in when you should tell them after you have made the decision that you want to get a divorce and, "When" as in what part of the hour, day or week do you tell them.

When clients call us for our divorce service, many have already discussed getting a divorce with their spouse, but many others have not and they will ask me what I think is the best time to tell their spouse. I tell them that it is better to talk to their spouse about wanting a divorce before any actual court documents start flying around. I think the conversation should come first and the actual filing of divorce papers should come after. So what I am recommending is that when you talk to your spouse that you are not there to hand them any type of divorce papers. It will be overwhelming enough to have the conversation and you are going to want to focus on just the conversation and not be distracted by court documents.

I recommend telling your spouse soon after you have made the decision that you absolutely want to get divorced. When you know for certain that you want a divorce, that is the time to tell them. Here is what you have to watch out for if you hold off or wait. You are going to have this thought of having to tell them on your mind constantly until you tell them. It will consume you and you will be thinking about it all day and night and it will effect you. The other thing you need to be mindful of is that you may start to look for things they are doing wrong more often or frequently, in more of a coping method for you to make them out to be the bad person so it makes it easier for you to break the news. While this may work in helping make them the bad person, it will certainly effect the delivery of the news to them. You may have this sick feeling in your stomach as you wait to tell them. The longer you wait the more you will feel this sick feeling. I can tell you from experience that my clients feel a sense of relief once their feelings are out in the open and they have discussed this with their spouse.

The other "when" is time of the hour, day or week. Think of your normal schedule and try to find the right time. It might be better to wait until your spouse has unwound from work for a while, but before they start into their glass of wine or beer. This discussion is best done sober, and that goes for both of you. If you are going to have a cocktail, have it after you guys have talked. Do you tell them on a weekend or weekday? Is it better that you have the discussion on a weekday where at least during the day you are not together and risk the chances of fighting? Maybe right after discussing this it is best to have a little space between you. Or maybe you would rather discuss this on the weekend where you do have additional time to talk and discuss the details of the divorce. You will have to make a judgment call.

Now, when you have figured out when you are going to talk to your spouse, what words are you going to use? How are you going to start the conversation? My recommendation is to think of it as firing an employee. I am not trying to diminish the circumstances, just trying to put this in perspective of the type of tone you need to have. When you are going to fire an employee, you don't start talking about all the things they have done and provide reasons and examples or apologize or provide excuses.

You just say, "you're fired" or "I have to let you go". I prefer the latter of those examples. The divorce equivalent of those phrases is, "I want a divorce" and "I can't be married to you anymore". Again, I like the second one better than the first. The direct route is going to serve you well in this situation and you need to get right to the point. "I wanted to speak to you because I need to tell you that I can't be married to you anymore".

What To Say After Telling Your Spouse You Want A Divorce

Here is what I tell my clients. Once you have told your spouse you want a divorce, explain to them that you want to try to figure out everything without having to hire an attorney. Tell them that you don't want to spend a ton of money on your divorce and that you want to try and work it out amicably. If you guys can at least agree to not use attorneys, you have a good chance of getting through the divorce process on your own with a non-attorney legal service provider like ours.

I then tell them, when they are ready, to make sure that their spouse is directed to our website or to call me so I can have a discussion with them to try to explain the process. I want them to know we are a neutral third party, not here to take sides or represent either party, rather just here to help facilitate the divorce process the best we can. The biggest thing I can help with this at this moment is to put the other spouse's concerns at ease as quickly as possible.

Don't Listen To Your Friends

You remember the last time you purchased a car? Then all of a sudden you start seeing that car everywhere? In a similar fashion, once you start going through the divorce process you will undoubtedly start talking about it and whether you want it or not, your friends, relatives and even strangers will start to give you advice and commentary. Anything from, "you need an attorney" to "I got screwed in my divorce". People have their opinions and experiences with divorce, but their negative experiences is not what you have to go through.

You and your spouse are in control of the outcome of your divorce. How it starts and how it ends. In my experience, speaking to your friends about your divorce or asking them for advice is generally a bad idea. Nothing ever comes good of it and everything they are telling you is filtered by them. We all rely on friends and family when going through times like these, so I can't expect you to listen to me, a stranger, so I will leave you with something you hopefully follow. Take what your friends say with a grain of salt. Listen to them, but then come to your own conclusions.

Fear

To be sure, getting a divorce is going to change your life one way or another and by how much will vary from person to person. But with change, comes fear. Fear of the unknown mostly. Fear of change. But don't let fear overpower you or cause you to make rash decisions. Here is where I am going with on this.

When I was talking to you about not listening to your friends and to come to your own conclusions, I was referring to people who will either purposely or with the best of intensions, cause a certain level of fear in you. Specifically by stating that if you don't get an attorney that you will get screwed in your divorce. I am using that language purposely, because that is usually how I hear it being stated by my clients so perhaps this terminology rings true for you too.

I am also talking about the fear attorneys will try to instill in you as well with similar rhetoric. Let me tell you how this works. You decide you want to speak to an attorney about your divorce.

Let's say you have some questions, which is fine. What most attorneys will do is tell you all the bad things that can happen to you if you don't hire an attorney and why you need to retain them now to "protect your rights".

You want to know why attorneys say this? Because they have to. They have to tell you all this scary stuff because it is their job to "fight for your rights". It is their job to get you the "best deal" in your divorce. It is not that they are bad, necessarily, just that the very nature of having an attorney puts you in an adversarial position with your spouse. I mean it is called, "The Adversarial System". I don't want to go to far with this conversation because I have dedicated an entire chapter to this.

What I wanted you to get out of this chapter is that there is a better way. You don't have to go down the path of the adversarial system. You don't have to go to court, you don't have to go to trial, you don't even need to see a courtroom. I laugh to myself sometimes because when people call me they frequently will ask, "What would a judge say about (blank)". And my answer is always the same. No judge is ever going to make a decision about anything if you guys can work out your agreements outside of court. The only people who ever see a judge are the ones that could not figure it out by themselves and needed to have a judge to decide. There is a big misconception that to get divorced that you need to go in front of a judge for them to make a decision.

This is so far from the truth. My clients who use our service and ultimately come to an agreement will never set foot in court. My office deals directly with the spouses to come to an agreement and document that agreement. This turns the divorce process into more of simply drafting agreements and submitting them to the court for approval. The Court does not look at your agreements to see if anything is fair or even equal. All they care is to make sure that the children are being taken care of and that procedure was followed property and the divorce paperwork done correctly. That's it.

Here is how you get rid of fear about divorce and the divorce process. Get educated. You are taking a great first step here by reading this book. You can also go to my website at www.divorce661.com and read the over 2,000 articles, videos and podcasts I have produced on the topic of divorce in California. You can also just pick up the phone and call 661-281-0266 for a free phone consultation where I can learn about your situation, discuss if our services are a good fit for you and answer any questions you have about divorce and the divorce process.

Chapter 3

TRUE COST OF DIVORCE

Unless you know someone who has gone through divorce who has talked about how much money they have spent on their divorce, you won't believe me. But I am just going to come out and say it. The average cost of divorce is $30,000. That is $30,000 per person. Go ahead, do your own research and Google it... When you're done with this book that is.

The thing is, it does not matter if it is $30,000, $20,000, or $50,000, it is just a lot of money. I am not trying to argue my point for the $30,000 either, I just want to make sure I caught your attention at how much a divorce can cost. Now, you may be saying, "We'll, that is for highly contested cases that go to court". Some might be, but usually those types of cases go upwards of $60,000 to $100,000. I know you don't believe me. It's okay. Let's just agree that divorce can be expensive. I can live with that and we can still be friends.

In this chapter I am going to explain to you why using an attorney for your divorce can be so expensive. I am going to discuss ways of saving money (in the event you do actually need an attorney) and how attorneys bill you. I am going to walk you through the process of calling an attorney, going to the consultation and reviewing the attorney retainer agreement.

What I am about to share with you is one of the most widely misunderstood issues of hiring an attorney. And this is the topic of how attorney retainers work.

Now, we are talking about divorce attorney retainers here as that is where my experience has been first hand. I am going to share with you how people quickly get in over their heads, spend way more money than they wanted or knew was being spent and how all that happens. Essentially, I am going to pull back the curtain on how the process of working with attorneys works.

The Attorney Consultation

Depending on the size of the law firm and how they work organizationally, you may never be able to get the attorney on the phone or even have contact with them until you have agreed to pay for a consultation. This is how it was when I worked for a large family law firm. The attorneys did not answer the "intake calls". This is what it is called when someone calls for the first time. It was the Paralegal's job to field these initial intakes and get the persons information, see what issues they are having and then set the appointment for the attorney consultation. It always amazed me because people would be willing pay as much as $300 (a reduced rate for the consultation) without ever speaking with the attorney they were going to consult with prior. I must have just been that good on the phone. ;) Now, if you happen to be working with an attorney that does not have a staff, known as a sole-practitioner, you will have better luck actually having a conversation with them on the phone before committing to the paid consultation.

Pay For Your Attorney Consultation

That's right. I recommend you always pay for your attorney consultation. While there are ways of obtaining a free consultation sometimes, I would suggest that you pay for it. The quality of the consultation will be 100% better. Here is why. When you go on a free consultation with an attorney (usually by referral from your local BAR association) the attorneys know that these referrals are generally low quality leads. Not that you are low quality, but that the conversion rate of consultation to someone retaining is very low and it is usually someone just wanting free advice, and so that is how you're treated.

Additionally, the free consultations are only ½ hour and because you are not paying for it, the attorney is not going to want to give too much free legal advice and will spend much of their time trying to sell you on why you should retain them. I honestly believe that a free attorney consultation is worth every penny and you are wasting your time.

You can turn the tables on this by paying for the consultation. Here is why. You are paying for the attorneys time so you are in control. You have essentially retained them for an hour so they are working for you. I am not trying to make it sound like you can kick them around, but you are in more control and you will have a much more productive consultation.

Have Your Questions Ready & Written Down

You are paying for it, make you're time well spent. I always tell people, including my clients, that if they are going to pay for an attorney consultation to write down their questions and be prepared. You can't go in and say, "tell me what I need to know" You need to go in there and make a presentation of the facts in your specific situation and then one-by-one ask the questions you want answered. Yes, this means you are going to have to do some research on the things that are important to you prior to showing up. If you think you are going to go in unprepared and walk away with all the answers you are looking for, you are wrong. All you will get is topical information that will not be specific answers to your questions. You can find all the "topical" issues online. Don't wast your time and money. Be prepared. Otherwise you will be right back there for another consultation or feel the need to retain them because you didn't get the answers you needed to make a decision on what to do.

How Attorney Retainers Work

So let's say that you actually need a divorce attorney. You have a terrible situation and there is no way around it. It happens and I hope I have not given the impression that I am flat out against attorneys or that they are bad. I am not. I am just against you using an attorney when it is not necessary and wasting your money when there is a much better way. That's all.

Enter the Attorney Retainer Agreement. You need to understand how the attorney retainer agreements work. There are many versions, however most attorney retainers should, at a minimum, state the reason for retaining, the retainer amount and what the hourly fees of the attorney or attorneys is, what the hourly fees of their staff is and what they charge for other services such as photocopies, sending or receiving faxes and sometimes just thinking about you.

An attorney retainer agreement can be several pages and confusing. Remember, these were written by attorneys. For some reason, people feel rushed to sigh the retainer agreements. When you are done with your consultation, one way or another, you are going to be asked if you want to retain their services. From my experience when working at a law firm, more people immediately retain than don't. I don't know the exact reason why or what actually happened behind the closed door, but if I had to guess, it would be something like this. You just spent an hour with someone telling them things you normally only tell your closest friends and they say they are going to help you with your problem. There is a trust, a bond, they make you feel safe (remember the chapter on fear?) Maybe this is why people retain. It isn't because they wan't to throw down $5,000 on the retainer i can tell you that.

So what should you do? Take the retainer agreement home and read it. Maybe that's the time you should talk to a friend or family member. Read it! Sleep on it. Maybe you want to consult with another attorney first. when you have bought or sold a home did you hire the first realtor? No, you probably (or should have) interviewed a few different realtors. There is no rush. In most cases there is no emergency. Now is the time to take a step back and think about things. Your mind is already going in one thousand different directions. Maybe after you've slept on it, perhaps the attorney will be willing to reduce their hourly rates. Never know, but worth asking.

The Evergreen Attorney Retainer Agreement

If you were reading the last section and breezed through what I said, please don't do that here. If you are going to retain an attorney, you need to know if it has what is known as an "Evergreen Clause". The word evergreen is probably not known to you, but it has many meanings. For instance, in the marketing world, say when I write this book, or when I write a blog post, to write "evergreen content" is to write things that will never change with time. The information is just as good now as it will be in 5 years, for example. The word "Evergreen" then means "to continue or go on and have no end". Evergreen plants are always green. You get the point.

An evergreen clause in an attorney retainer agreement means that you are retaining the attorney and, with some variance, that the agreement continues beyond the initial retainer amount you paid.

Here, it might be better to explain in context. Let's say you sign an evergreen attorney agreement. Again, this just means that there is a paragraph that says the agreement will continue on and not expire until you tell the attorney you no longer want them to represent you.

What I am about to tell you comes from personal experience so I am not getting this second hand or from reading it someplace else. So you retain the attorney and give them $5,000 (I will have an entire discussion on this). Your attorney then gets to work for you. You are probably thinking that they will call you when your retainer is almost gone to let you know that you will have to pay more money if they continue with your case. But this is not what happens. What happens is that your $5,000 is spent and when it is gone, they just keep on working on your case. When the $5,000 is gone, they don't tell you, and next thing you know you get a bill at the end of the month for the overages.

In my experience most people are shocked to realize that their retainer is gone in less than 30 days and they owe, at a minimum, another $5,000 already from what the law firm spent in addition. Clients would get upset, but the attorneys would simply say they had to do what was in their (the clients) best interest in "protecting their rights" and that is was necessary to do what they did and by the way... Did you read your attorney retainer agreement? No, you probably signed it right there in the law office and did not review it. That is what they are counting on and that is why law firms make so much money and why divorce is so expensive.

This happened so much with the law firm I worked with that I knew that at the end of the month, that by about the 3rd of each month when the billing statements reached their clients, that the phones would ring off the hook with complaints about how much their bill was and that they thought they had paid the $5,000 to take care of their divorce. Nope!

We had more people say they wanted to speak to their spouse to work out an agreement as soon as they received their first invoice. All of a sudden they wanted to settle their case with as little attorney involvement as possible. The true cost of divorce finally hit them. The sad thing is that so little was accomplished with the money they had already spent that it really didn't do them any good. This is why I tell people to explore their options before hiring an attorney for their divorce.

How Do The Costs Add Up So Fast?

It is all about billing. Everyone from the secretary on down is rated on how many hours they billed clients. Bill a ton and get accolades. Have low billing hours and next thing you know your job is on the line. But what are you billed for? Everything, and I mean everything.

You are billed when you email the attorney or their staff. You are billed for them to read it and to reply. You are billed for them writing letters on your behalf and you are billed for the paper the letters are written on and the photocopies they make and for the postage to get that letter where it is going. You are billed for everything. The minute any single staff member thinks about your file, you are being billed. It truly is a racket and in my opinion unethical, but you are the one that signed the agreement. The thing is, they wouldn't do it if they didn't get away with it, but they do. Not all the time mind you. Sometimes a client will complain to the BAR association and the attorneys have to account for their billing and it usually is reduced.

And guess what happens if you don't pay your bill after they have run up the charges on you? If you don't pay they will sue you. Yep. I have seen it so many times. First, they love you and want to "fight for your rights" but the second you don't pay them, they drop you like a bad habit, then sue you for what they owe. I honestly don't know how people that do these things sleep at night.

Keep in mind that they are not all like this. I know several attorneys that I have the highest regard for. Whenever my clients need legal advice or an attorney I always steer them to the attorneys I know do not do what I just discussed. I even tell people that absolutely need an attorney and can't use our service to call me so I can at least refer them to a good divorce attorney.

What Is The Average Cost Of Retainers?

As much as they can get! Not really true, but sort of. But there is an average for the area you live in. For instance, in and around the Los Angeles area you are looking at a retainer of at least $5,000 for the most generic cast. But the retainer does not matter. Why? Because the retainer is not the total cost of your divorce. There are so many factors to consider.

I always laugh when someone calls my office, thinking we are a law firm, and their very first questions to me is, "what is your retainer?" and my answer is, "what does that matter?" Usually they hang up, and that's okay because they would never become a client anyways, but the issues is that the amount of the retainer has no meaning. Does that mean that an attorney that has a $2,500 retainer is cheaper than one with a $5,000 retainer? No!

You have to understand what the purpose of the retainer is. I call it, "the getting started money" because it is in no way the "getting your case finished money". No It is just a portion of what you will be out of pocket to get started on your divorce case. Please understand that the retainer is not what they are saying it will take to complete to your divorce case. The attorney has to make a judgment call. They just spoke to you about what you have going on. They now know what you do for a living and what your spouse does for a living. They probably know what each of you make, because you told them, and they can probably guess at what they can get out of you for a retainer. You see, the more they get out of you for an initial retainer, the more they can bill before having to send you an invoice.

Here is the difference. Let's say they take a $10,000 retainer vs. a $5,000 retainer. The money goes in a trust account and it is not really theirs until they have billed for it. Usually monthly. So if they bill the $10,000, they can actually put it into their bank account if they had the $10,000 retainer. However, If they only charged you a $5,000 retainer but billed $10,000, they only put $5,000 in their pocket and are waiting for payment from you.

So the attorneys will always try to determine what they can get out of you for a retainer. The more the better for them, however they have to consider this with the fact that they may scare you off with a much larger retainer and that you may be, "retainer shopping". For this reason, you may find them requesting what your area averages for retainers.

The Retainer Is Not The Final Cost For Your Case

I hate to harp on this, but it is such a bad thing for people that I really want you to be aware of it. I can't tell you how many clients put down $5,000 for a retainer thinking that the money would get their case completed. I have had super easy cases where the spouses are in agreement spend $5,000 on an attorney and all that has happened is that the case was filed and nothing more. It was a complete waste of money. Then they had to end up hiring us anyways. I just hate to see that and I see it way to often, despite trying to get the word out to folks.

Large Law Firms vs. Solo-Practitioners

One of the decisions you will have to make is if you want to hire a larger law firm or a solo-practitioner. A large law firm is usually going to be more costly in the end from my experience. Here is my take on things. You are hiring someone to help you with your divorce. It is very personal and you only want to explain your circumstances to a few people. When you work for a large law firm, your file will be dropped down to an associate attorney who may or may not have the experience to work your case. The firm will sell you on the fact that this is to your benefit because a junior, less expensive attorney, is working your file thus saving you money. It just does not work out that way. While the junior attorney is working the file, they have to go to the partner attorney for advice so often that you might as well have a skilled solo-practitioner attorney that you like and can talk to. Do you really want to consult with one attorney then have to deal with their underlings?

With Solo-Practitioners, you will be working with the attorney at every stage. Most likely when you call, you will get them. Or not if they are in court. But you will just have to deal with that. In my business, I am the face of the company. I am who people talk to when they first call. I am the one they watched the video of who convinced them to use our company for their divorce. To pass them off would not be appreciated i'm sure. This is a very personal experience. I definitely have an opinion on the matter and that is to find an attorney you like. And if they are part of a larger law firm, just make sure that they will have a personal interest and be the ones working your case.

How To Keep Your Attorney Costs Down

This will be the last section on attorneys and then we are going to move on. I wanted this book to be about how there is a better option, but for those who are not aware of how things work, It would not make sense to tell you about a better solution without discussing the other issues when you decide to use an attorney.

Again, assuming you absolutely need an attorney, how can you save money? This is a good question and one that I discuss when my clients when their divorce case gets out of hand and we need to refer them to an attorney because their spouse has started doing things that harms who we are working with.

If you want to keep your costs down with your attorney, you need to make that well known up front. You need to tell them that you want to know what they are going to do before they do it. And most importantly, you need to ask them why they need to do it and how it will benefit you. More of your money is spent by the attorney making decisions on your behalf, which you gave them permission to do when you retained them. So make sure you lay down the ground rules before they spend your money. I have seen attorneys do things more from a billing standpoint that what is necessary. There is a lot of waste of money when you have an attorney. Make sure to protect yourself from this happening by making sure you and your attorney are on the same page.

Even If You Need An Attorney, Start With A Legal Document Assistant

I have people call our office and explain their situation to me all the time. I have to make a decision if their circumstances would be a good fit for our divorce service. In some cases, they will explain a situation that makes it apparent the they will need an attorney at some point. This is usually because the other spouse is behaving in a way that they actually do need attorney representation. These are generally divorce situation where one spouse has taken all the money, closed bank accounts, removed the spouse from health insurance or moved out and took the kids. These types of situations will need the advice and representation of a divorce attorney because this is a divorce case that is headed straight to court.

However, this does not mean that you can't use a Legal Document Assistant to get your divorce case started. I tell people that are in these situations to use our divorce service even if they know they will need an attorney. We save people so much money in the early phases of the divorce process. Let me explain.

When I worked for a divorce attorney the retainer was usually $5,000. This money was usually spent in the first 30 days and the divorce case had hardly even been started. Usually all that had happened is that the divorce case was filed, there were conversations between attorneys, perhaps a few letters back and forth, a few emails and meetings with you. I get calls all the time with people telling me that they spent $5,000 on a divorce attorney and that their divorce case was not finished. I look at their case summary with the court and can see that the case was just filed and nothing else happened. They are shocked to realize that they are nowhere close to being finished.

In the worst of situations, I see people spend all the money they had on an attorney and now the divorce case is finally going to trial and they can't afford to keep their attorney. So now, at the point they need their attorney the most, they no longer can afford them and have to face going to trial on their own.

So what I tell people, regardless if they absolutely know they will need a divorce attorney, is to start their divorce case with us. We can prepare and file you divorce case, have your spouse served and complete all your financial disclosures. I estimate that with the work that we do in the initial phases of the divorce process that we save our clients about $5,000 in attorney's fees. Save this money up front so you can spend the money later on an attorney when you actually need them to give you legal advice and represent you in court. The beginning of the divorce process is purely paperwork. You don't need legal advice for that. At www.divorce661.com we can help you file your divorce case anywhere in California so make sure to give us a call.

Chapter 4

RESPONSIBILITY

I have an excuse for everything and am probably no different than most people. It is almost instinctual thinking. For instance, since staring my divorce business I have gone from weighing 200 pounds to now weighing 274 pounds. Why did this happen? We'll it's obvious. I started a business and had to work so much that I couldn't find time to continue working out. That is what I told myself. The real reason is that I stopped making time to go to the gym. I stopped eating as well as I was and maybe, just maybe, started drinking a few beers each night when I got home after a long day at the office.

The good news is that I realized that I had to get back into the gym and start eating better and thankfully the weight is coming off. But you see how easy it is to make an excuse rather than ask yourself what the real reason something is happening? This is the type of thinking I am talking about. You can take almost any situation and find an excuse. It is hard to ask yourself, "what could I do different" or "how am I responsible for this?"

Sometimes it is hard to take responsibility. Let me take that back. It is always hard to take responsibility. It is usually just easier to make an excuse or blame someone else. It seems society as a whole does not accept responsibility for the things that

30

happen. This is just as true in divorce. If you think about it, just about everything in life that happens to us, happens due to some action or inaction. Something we did or didn't do is the reason things happen, good or bad. Yes, there are other "reasons" things happen, but we can control much of how things end up.

As you consider divorce or go through the divorce process, I encourage you to try and accept responsibility for where you are at. Sure, there is a "reason" you are getting divorced. Most of our clients fall into one of a couple of situations. First, there is the obvious "who is at fault" clients where one spouse cheated on the other spouse or did "something" that both spouses can point to and say that is the reason they are getting divorced. Second, we have our clients who have just grown apart or where one spouse wants the divorce and the other does not.

Lets take a look at each of these scenarios from a perspective of responsibility. And I am talking about responsibility from both spouses. Now, in this first group, where the spouses can both point to this one "thing" that occurred to be the reason for the divorce. I want to explain how each spouse can take responsibility and this will best be achieve by telling a story and showing the choices you have.

First, lets talk about the spouse who did the "thing" that is the cause of the divorce. Lets say the husband had an affair. Going back to having excuses for everything, the husband would probably placing blame on his spouse as the reason it happened. Reasons such as, "she stopped taking care of herself" or "she does not make time for me" or whatever the reason is. But these are not reasons, they are excuses.

Now, when someone does something bad to another, as in this scenario, the spouse that harmed the other will usually find fault with the other spouse. Meaning they will start to make less of the other spouse. It is almost like a coping mechanism for the person who did something bad. They know they are in the wrong and so that they don't feel the guilt of what they did, they will make less or find fault with the other spouse so they feel better about themselves. This is the opposite of taking responsibility.

For the spouse that was cheated on, the first thing you are going to want to do is to blame. Seems a normal reaction. Of course you will be mad and hurt over the broken trust and promises. I am not going to come out and say that you are at fault for the other spouse cheating. However, the cheating was most likely the end result, the final act if you will, of a relationship that had broken down one way or another. Meaning that there might have been things you could have done, perhaps, that would have prevented something like this to happen. Maybe there was nothing. I am just saying to take a look and think about it. See if there is something, anything you could have done different that would have possibly changed tings. I want to be clear. I am in no way saying that anyone is responsible for their spouse cheating, except for the one who cheated.

In this scenario, there is going to be some upset, anger and maybe even hate. I have to tell you that I have dealt with clients in this exact situation many times and I have seen spouses handle their divorce very badly and have seen them handle it well. As well as divorce can be in these situations. Let's take a look at two ways this can be handled, and this comes from personal experience.

I remember this one divorce case very well. I was working for a family law firm and the wife retained the law firm I was working for. Their situation was that wife stayed home and took care of the two children while the husband worked. I would say this is fairly typical situation, but not as much anymore these days with both spouses working. The husband had cheated on the wife and the wife wanted to get revenge. She told the attorney that she wanted to make him pay for what he did and try to ruin him financially.

She asked the attorney to make his life miserable and to get as much money out of him as possible. With her goal to get as much money out of him, she fought to have full legal and physical custody of their children. She wanted to move away, out of the State, so he could not see the children. This divorce case could have gone much differently, but she let her emotions get the better of her and they ended up at multiple trials. They went to trial over child support, spousal support, over her request to move out of state and to try to keep the children from him. It was very sad to see.

All that will come of this is a relationship that will be toxic the rest of their lives. It is not as if they won't see each other after the divorce. At the time, they had two young children, less than 5 years old. Remember, if you have children, you are going to see your ex for the foreseeable future. Whether it be at custody exchanges, school plays, graduations or birthdays, they are going to be in your life.

Taking Responsibility

I always say that it is easy to hire an attorney for your divorce. Throw some money at your problem and let someone else deal with it. That is what the attorneys do after all. It is harder to take responsibility and handle your own divorce. A few pages back I was talking about the spouse that wanted to ruin her husband and exact revenge. Let me give you another example. In a very similar situation as the one described above, except that the roles were reversed. In this case the wife did the cheating and instead of deciding to use an attorney for their divorce, they decided to use our divorce service.

The wife who had cheated took responsibility for her actions and owned up to it. The husband, who was very upset, knew he could no longer live with her for doing what she did, but said despite what had happened that they both needed to be responsible as they too had two young children.

So I guided them through the divorce process. We met several times together and got them eventually sorted out. I could see that it was hard on both of them. One accepted that she created the situation they were in and the other took responsibility for making sure that the family ended up as well as possible on the other end of the divorce. They were able to come to an agreement on the child custody and visitation. They were able to agree to spousal support and child support. They were eventually able to agree on everything. They now have a co-parenting schedule with their children who will benefit from their parents being as amicable as possible with each other despite how their marriage ended. Don't you think this

When Spouses Grow Apart

Next, lets talk about the folks who just grew apart. In my line of work this is more common than anything else. Don't get me wrong, I never ask why people are getting a divorce, but some people just feel the need to tell me.

I know you have probably read somewhere that the biggest cause for getting a divorce is when someone cheats. But in my experience over the years, the biggest cause of divorce is spouses just growing apart.

It is not just that they grew apart. That is just an excuse. The reason they grew apart is because they stopped doing the things that once made them want to be together. I think the words we will use here is that they got comfortable and stopped creating together. I think that we are all guilty of this.

I am going to get a little opinionated here. I don't think that spouses just grow apart. I think that growing apart happens over time and is the fault of both involved. Talking about responsibility, this falls on the shoulders of both spouses. Unlike the previous situation where one of the spouses did something wrong, I think that when spouses grow apart that they are both responsible.

I am not a marriage counselor by any means, but I have seen and spoke to more than my fair share of people going through divorce that say they just grew apart. What I learned by talking to 100's of clients who say this, there is a common theme. At some point, they just started slowly living separate lives. They had not done things together for a while. The husband started spending more time in front of the TV or began drinking a little more. The wife started going out more with friends without her husband. I could give a ton of examples, but the issue is that they stopped being a unit working together and started doing their own thing.

This then evolved into not helping each other out, such as with household duties or even being considerate of each other. Eventually they stopped celebrating birthdays and anniversaries and later forgot when their anniversary was. Think I am kidding? Some of my clients who say they have just grown apart often have to confer with one another to figure out the date of marriage when we are trying to fill out their divorce paperwork.

I was explaining in the beginning of the book that it is almost like the men feel that to provide a roof over the heads of their wife and children and provide a safe environment is enough. This is probably a topic that has enough content for another book that could be written. Perhaps that will be my next book!

But this is how women explain this to me. I hear this all the time when women are explaining to me why they are just not happy anymore, that their spouse did not do anything in particular, just that they are not happy. They tell me that their husband is happy the way things are, but that they are not. They say their relationship seems stagnant and feels more like a business partnership than a marriage. If you ask me, I would tell you that our needs are just different.

I know that I have taken responsibility for this in my marriage. It is sort of a funny story actually. I was explaining this very situation with my wife several months ago. I began telling her what the women's complaints were about their spouse and just not being happy with how their relationship is and how their husbands seem fine with how the relationship is.

She then tells me that I could use some work in that department as well. It was a real eye opener for me because I thought everything was great. Sound familiar? What's more is that, even though I was hearing this complaint every day, that I thought I was except, that this is not how I was at all. So even though I was being told every day these things, I still didn't see that I was doing the same thing in many regards.

You see I personally feel that I am very considerate. Meaning, I try to do things that my wife would appreciate. I get her flowers for no reason other than to tell her I love her. I go out of my way to do things I know she would appreciate. Let me give you some examples. My wife travels quite a bit for work and last year she was in Chicago on assignment which happened to fall on our anniversary. So I surprised her by having flowers delivered to her room.

Then later that week on Friday she was returning from Chicago. I checked my flight tracker application on my phone to see where she was and it showed that she had landed. This was impossible because she was not due to land for another 2 hours and I thought she had a direct flight. When I looked at where she was it said Las Vegas. So I sent her a text and said, "Are you in Vegas" and she said she was and still on the plane because it was just a 30 minute layover. I told her, "get off the plane!" She didn't believe I was serious. I finally convinced here to get off the plane in Las Vegas and told her I would drive up to meet her. So in that instant, at about 2pm in the afternoon on a Friday, I dropped everything and grabbed some clothes and was in Las Vegas 4 hours later. We had a great weekend and drove home together on Sunday. I posted these things on Facebook and got good responses from my friends so I thought I was doing pretty darn good.

Come to think of it, she is currently in New York for a week as I write this and will be coming back Friday which is our anniversary. I will have something nice set up for when she returns.

One more example, I promise. Just a few weeks ago, my wife was in Seattle on a project that was supposed to last just one week. On Friday she learned she needed to stay until the following Wednesday. She was going to fly home that Friday and then go back up on Monday, but the problem was that she would have had to go out Sunday morning as there were no flights going out Monday morning early enough for her to be there in time. So that meant that she would get home late Friday night and turn around and leave Sunday morning. That didn't seem to make sense. So I told her to stay in Seattle and I flew out and made a last minute weekend of it and I returned on Monday. How thoughtful, right?

You know what? Come to think of it, all these things I was doing happened after we had our little discussion. But I think I would have done them anyways. Or maybe I have changed and actually listened to what she was telling me.

But going back to my conversation with my wife, I asked her what else I could do that she would appreciate. It turns out that all she wanted me to do is pick up on the things she says she has been wanting to do. I was confused because I didn't know there was anything she wanted to do that we were not doing. But apparently there was plenty.

She had mentioned several times that she wanted to go to a play in Los Angeles. She asked if I recalled her saying that which I did. I guess I just dismissed it because it was not something I necessarily wanted to do. You know what? As I am writing this, it is making me think of something else she has been mentioning. For at least the last 3 weeks she has been telling me she wants us to go to the Skyslide. The Skyslide is a outdoor slide on the 69th floor of the tallest building on the West Coast of the US Bank building in Los Angeles.

This is sad. Here I am writing this chapter and literally thoughts are going through my mind of examples where I am missing things my wife wants to do. Even though I have to hear how spouses are unhappy every day and think I am doing a pretty good job, I realize that I am missing the cues. They are not just cues, she has literally said to me three times, "I want us to go to the Skyslide." I guess it is a matter of what is important to me. I have to admit, going here is not something I really want to do. I am a little afraid of heights. But it is interesting sitting here realizing how easy it is to dismiss something our spouses say even when we are actively trying to take responsibility for ensuring we are both enjoying our marriage. All us men have a lot of work to do.

When Only One Spouse Wants The Divorce

The final sort of group of clients we get are those where only one spouse wants the divorce and the other spouse does not. These types of divorce cases are a little tricky to handle and everyone handles it differently. I am handling 3 divorce cases like this right now and will explain how each of them is taking responsibility or not. Really, the only difference between when spouses grow apart and when one spouse wants the divorce and the other spouse does not is that it is mutual when they grew apart and when one spouse does not want it, that spouse just didn't notice that they were growing apart.

I recently had a gentleman call to schedule a conference call between he and his wife to discuss our services. He indicated that they had discussed divorce and they just had a few questions. I get on the phone with them and be begins asking questions. About 3 minutes into the conversation his wife begins crying and asking him why he is doing this to her and why they are not going to try counseling. It was apparent that she was not ready for this call so I ended the call. She later called me separately to talk to me. She wanted to ask me what she should do if she didn't want the divorce.

I told her that in California there is no way to stop a divorce. If someone wants to divorce you, they can and don't have to have a reason. In California, we are considered a no-fault state which means you don't have to have a reason other than claiming irreconcilable differences. Depending on what State you live in, this could be different. Her response was that while she does not want the divorce she didn't see any point in trying to make it difficult so decided to just go along with the process.

On the other end of the spectrum, we sometimes see total unwillingness to cooperate or participate. In this next examples, this couple had been married for a short time and had no kids. They have actually been separated and living apart for about a year now. I asked if the spouse would be cooperative and he said he was not sure, but knew that she didn't want the divorce. I contacted her and advised what was going on and never heard from her again despite multiple attempts. And I get it. It is not something she wants to do. But what I want you to take away from this is that there is nothing that can be done to stop it, it only just makes the divorce process more difficult. Instead of this being done in an amicable way where she could just come to our office and sign a few forms, now we are going to have to have her served the divorce papers and complete their divorce case by default instead of it being by agreement. A default is just where one of the parties does not participate. We are always hoping to have our clients ultimately come to an agreement, but where one party just won't participate, we have to go by way of default.

The third current client we have, his wife wanted the divorce and said that they have grown apart, but the husband did not want the divorce. While he was not happy with her decision, he just said he does not want to be married to someone that doesn't want to be married to him. A simple approach, but respectable.

In my business I am mostly working with spouses who are trying to get through their divorce as best they can. They have taken the first step at responsibility by deciding, regardless of what got them here, that they are going to work together. That they are going to use a non-attorney divorce service to help them and that they don't want to hire attorneys or fight it out in court. If you are considering a divorce and you live in California, I would encourage you to give me a call so we can help you. You can learn more at www.divorce661.com.

Chapter 5

COMPROMISE

You are going to have to compromise if you expect to get through the divorce process amicably. Most of our clients are pretty good about working through the details of their divorce in regards to what they want to do with the kids and money decisions such as support and property and debt distribution. But where folks run into trouble, there is help. We always recommend professional mediation if you need someone in a room to help you through the decision making process. You can learn more about divorce mediation in chapter 7.

You know you are making compromises when it feels like you are giving more than you want and when you are not getting everything you would like. I tell my clients that it will feel this way when trying to make the decisions. Let me show you some examples of compromises that may come up in a divorce process.

Compromises In Regards To Your Home

When you go through a divorce you will be deciding how to split up your assets and debts and when it comes to the family home there are only three things that can happen. Only two really, but I want to talk about a third compromise we have done as well. Here they are. You can agree that one of you can keep the home or you can agree to sell it. In my experience it seems that there is always one spouse that wants to keep the family home. This is especially true if there are minor children involved. But keeping the family home may not be achievable for a few reasons which we will discuss.

One of the first things that you should determine is whether or not the spouse that wants to keep the home can make the payments. Remember, you are going to be living with less income in most cases. You are going from one or two incomes and one set of expenses, and now will have the same income, but two sets of expenses. The standard of living will usually change. Lets now assume that you can make the payment because perhaps you have owned the home for a while and the payment is lower than it would be to rent at current rates. We see this quite a bit currently.

But this presents a possible problem. If you have owned the home long enough or simply because of economics, there is equity in the home, you will have to decide how that equity will be split if you re not selling it. Obviously, the best way to achieve this is to refinance the home and pull money out to pay the portion to the other spouse. We find that in most cases, the spouse trying to refinance won't qualify on their income alone. Another option would be to just take out a second mortgage, but again this would cause your payment to go up and requires one to qualify.

Use Assets & Debts To Offset Equity

A principle I want you to remember is that not everything has to be split down the middle. You can use other assets or even debt to offset one or more assets to equalize what each of you are keeping.

Going back to the issue with the home. Lets say that you want to keep the home and there is $100,000 in equity. If you sold it, each of you would get $50,000. Assume you don't qualify for a refinance or 2nd mortgage on the home so it appears the only solution is to sell it. What I tell my clients is to try to find another asset or debt that could be used as an offset. In this example, lets say that the other spouse has a pension or 401k with $100,000 in it. You could compromise and have one spouse keep the house, along with it's equity and the other spouse could keep their pension and it becomes a fair tradeoff. Of course each situation is different so you will want to carefully negotiate these issues.

I actually just had a call from someone today that was looking to use our service. She said she had listened to my podcast at Divorce Master Radio on iTunes where I had discussed using debt to offset the home. Here is what she asked. She asked if her husband could keep her part of the equity and in exchange he also keep an extra, equal part of the community debt. The answer Is Yes! Problem solved.

One issue we see here is that the spouse moving out desires to have a little getting started money which would ordinarily come from the sale of the home so they can rent or purchase another residence. Just more things to consider. And remember, we are talking about compromising here. Everything does not have to work out exactly even. It should just be fair.

Outside Of The Box Compromises

We covered selling the home which is pretty straight forward and I showed you some ways to compromise when one of the spouses wants to keep the home. But what if non of that is possible? I wanted to tell you about an outside of the box agreement we have come up with as suggestions to some of our clients.

We had a couple agree that the wife would stay in the family home until the kids turned 18 and then they would sell the home at that time and split the proceeds. Both spouses did not want to uproot the children from their neighborhood or school so we helped them arrange a way for this to happen. What was decided upon was that the wife would stay in the home with the children and instead of the husband paying spousal support, he would pay the mortgage instead which would keep her in the home.

Compromises Related To Your Children

Did you know that the courts do not care about any of the decisions you make? They don't care who gets what assets or debts and they don't check to see that you split things evenly. They figure that if you guys have reached an agreement that you have done so in your best interest. They won't even interfere on how you decide to divide up time or custody of your children. If you guys agree that one spouse will have full legal and physical custody, they will not stop you. The only thing the courts actually do look at is to make sure that the children will taken care of financially.

There is a phrase I want you to remember. "The best interests of the children." This is a phrase the courts use in making any decision. If you guys are in agreement, no judge is going to change anything, but what I want to tell you is when working towards an agreement, start first by trying to figure out what would be in your children's best interest first, and yours second.

When I worked for the law firm I saw first-hand too many divorce cases where the spouses used the children as pawns, looked at them as money and used them to punish the other spouse. You will be serving your children well to make the decisions of custody and timeshare in their best interest.

Non-Specific Child Custody Plans / Co-Parenting

Many of our clients are not aware that they do not have to have an actual parenting plan in place with the courts. Yes, this is true and our clients are happy to hear this. What this means is that you don't have to have an actual schedule of who the children will be with on what days and what times. Let me give you example of the differences.

When I was at the law firm where people were fighting and using the children as pawns, they were fighting for every minute of time they can get with the children. Not necessarily because of their strong desire to be with them as much as it is so they can either pay less child support or receive more child support. It is sad. So what they then have is a super detailed child custody plan that accounts for every day, every hour, every holiday, I mean everything. It says who is dropping off and who it picking up and when and where. Child custody plans can get very ridiculous. But they don't have to be.

Because the courts do not require you to have a parenting plan in place whatsoever in California, many of our clients opt for a non-specific child custody plan. Some of our child custody agreements just say that the parents will share joint legal and joint physical custody. And that is it. No dates or times or even a percentage of time share is given. The idea behind doing this is that the parents don't feel the need to have a specified parenting plan because they are able to figure it out on an ongoing bases and don't need the court's intervention or court order for child custody. Other reasons for doing this is to have flexibility in their schedule for parents who may have alternating or changing work schedules such as Police, Fire, and other emergency workers.

While this is a very popular way of expressing the child custody of the children, keep in mind that if you decide to go this route that you have no real recourse if you and your spouse are at odds over a particular decision down the road. So you may want to consider having a few built in orders if you feel that would be necessary. Otherwise, your court order for custody is so open that there is nothing to enforce. You could not complain to the judge that he or she is not following the custody agreement because there literally is not one. I have only had one couple come back to me after they established a non-specific child custody order and later decided that they wanted to have some specifics included in areas they were frequently having disagreements on.

Agreements Don't Have To Be Equal

I had a client the other day tell me she and her husband were trying to figure out how to show to the court that the agreement they are making were equal. She said that they had an agreement but that when you looked at who was getting what, that one of them was receiving more in assets than the other and they were concerned that the judge would not approve their agreement. Two thing on this point. One, I already stated that the courts do not look at your agreements to see if they are fair. They don't care. Second, when we prepare your final agreements, known at the judgment or settlement agreement, we do not include the values of the assets or debts each of your are keeping. I explained this to our client and she was relieved to learn that they don't have to have a 50/50 split of their assets and debts.

I will tell you that more times than not, the agreement that we are drafting for our clients are not 50/50 agreements. Our clients are usually pretty good about compromising. For instance, lets say that both the spouses have a pension or 401k in their name. And normally you would each split half of each others plan. Many times our clients are simply saying that they each agreed to keep their own pension, even though the values were not the same. Sometimes it was part of an equity swap as discussed above and sometimes it was just the agreement that they made. As an example, I have clients right now where one is a Fire

Fighter and the other a Teacher. The Teacher had been working much longer and had much more in her pension than the Fire Fighter. Despite that, they each simply agreed to keep their own pension.

That is the benefit of working with our company and handling your divorce without attorneys and without the court's involvement. You get to make all the decisions and there is no limit to the types of arrangement you can come up with. You and your spouse, as well as your children, will come out much better on the other end of the divorce if you work collaboratively to come up with your agreements.

Chapter 6

LEGAL DOCUMENT ASSISTANTS

I want to answer the question of what a Legal Document Assistant is because I am always getting the question from people going through divorce on how we are able to handle divorce cases without being attorneys. I am going to give you my version of it and not the legal mumbo jumbo version of it.

If you have never heard the words, "Legal Document Assistant" before you are not alone. The various associations have done a terrible job of promoting the industry as a whole and the folks out there operating LDA business are stuck in the stone age. The Legal Document Assistant profession is so unknown that I didn't even want to use it in the title of this book. I think people would have thought to themselves, "what the hell is that" and just move on.

This is my explanation of what Legal Documents Assistants do in the most simplistic form. We do what attorneys do, we just don't give legal advice or represent people in court. Depending on the skill level of the LDA, you can attorney quality assistance. This means we don't represent either party and show you how to take a legal advantage over your spouse.

We do handle all matters of legal filings, my company, www.divorce661.com specializes in divorce and other family law related matters. This means we handle divorce cases of course, but we also help people obtain spousal support orders, child custody and support orders and anything else related to a divorce or family law related matter. We even handle contested cases when the spouses are not in agreement and they can't afford to hire an attorney. I honestly don't like to handle those types of cases, that's why I stopped going to law school as it was just not my thing. But I do handle them because it is the right thing to do when someone does not have the money to hire an attorney, but need attorney quality work done for them. The only real difference is that when it comes time for a court hearing, they will be the ones going to the hearing by themselves, unless they hire an attorney on a short term basis as we discussed before with the limited scope representation.

Paralegals Are Not Legal Document Assistants

When I am making the distinction between paralegals and Legal Document Assistants, keep in mind that I am referring to California Law's only. I don't know how it works in other states except to say that Legal Document Assistants are only in 5 states currently in the US. So paralegals may or may not be a solution in other states.

Now, I will assume you have heard of the word paralegal. A Paralegal is someone who works under the supervision of an attorney. A Paralegal cannot handle a divorce case or contract to do business with a client directly. The attorney gets the client and the paralegal does the work under their supervision. A Paralegal cannot own a "paralegal business" or offer services directly to clients, at least in California. Despite these rules, there are more "Paralegals" running illegal businesses than there are actual Registered Legal Document Assistants. I have to deal with this every day.

The problem with these illegal businesses is that there is a reason they are not registered Legal Document Assistants. To be a Legal Document Assistant you have to have a combination of a college degree, working under the supervision of an attorney and / or working for the courts. I actually have done all three and believe that I am the only Legal Document Assistant in California that has worked for the Superior Court Systems in California. These "paralegals" are not trained and provide a sub-par service. Usually what happens is that they lure you in with a ridiculously low fee for service (as that is their only marketing advantage) and then realize that they don't have the ability to complete your divorce case.

It is so frustrating to have to take the call from the client who tried to use another "cheaper" service, not knowing that they were not a legitimate service and then have to spend 30 minutes explaining that we are fully in compliance and have the skills, training and experience required to successfully complete their divorce case regardless of the circumstances. Evidence of this is that ½ of our business comes from people who were not able to get their divorce case completed correctly by a paralegal company or that once they paid them, they never heard from the person again.

Let me give you an example this just happened yesterday afternoon. It was about 3:30 p.m., and I received a call from a gentleman that said he had started his divorce about 8 months ago, "with some paralegal company". The first thing I did was ask him who he had decided to use and he told me. Right there on the phone I looked up who this paralegal company was and the issues were immediately obvious. The first thing I noticed is that they did not have a website. This was a huge red flag. The only trace of them I could find is a Google listing.

When I get these calls, and as I stated, I get them a lot, my first instinct is to tell these callers that they should make the company they paid do the work they were hired to do, which is what I told this gentleman. He then said that he has had such a terrible experience with them that he just wanted to come in so I could take care of this divorce paperwork.

When he showed up I started looking through the paperwork that they had completed. I was completely shocked. They had prepared all of the paperwork incorrectly. Not just some of it, all of it. But that was not the worst thing that I learned. It turns out that he had been emailing them repeatedly and would not get a response. Not until he threatened to make a complaint did they even return his email. Oh, by the way, I should mention that the only reason he only kept emailing then and not calling them is because they said they don't accept phone calls from existing clients, only new potential clients. As he told me on the phone, "they answered the phone and were quick to take my money when I hired them, but after that I couldn't get ahold of them."

He then showed me the emails he has received from them. Just unbelievable. They were telling him that certain documents were filed with the court and he just had to wait. Not true. I showed him right there in my office the Superior Court website that shows the documents that had been filed and it was apparent that they were not being honest with him. As I got further into reviewing his documents, it turns out that we had to completely start over. I am talking about starting over from square one and re-filing his Petition for divorce because the mistakes were so bad that the way the divorce case was filed, it would never be approved by the court.

Now, he and his wife were amicable, but when we conferenced in his soon to be ex wife, she completely lost it and broke down crying on the phone. She could not believe that they had to start the divorce case from scratch again. The paralegal company they hired had made such a bad mistake on the original filing that we had to start all over again.

He later told me that he was referred to that particular paralegal company by a co-worker who was also going through divorce. He said she was having the same problems not being able to get in touch with or finalizing her divorce.

He calls her from my office and explains to her what happened to his divorce case. She then provides me her divorce case and I look it up online. Guess what? Same exact problem, except her case had been going on for more than a year and a half and was stopped at the exact same point. Both of them were thoroughly disappointed. She also has an appointment with our office tomorrow so we can get working on her divorce case as well. This was a complete waste of time and their money and as I stated before frustrates me about the type of businesses we have to deal with. I would say, "businesses in our industry", but they are not. They should not even be in business.

Because of what they had been through I gave them a hefty discount on our fees and I sat there for several hours and completed his entire divorce case for him right there on the spot. I wanted to make sure he knew that there were true professionals like us that are here to help him.

I wish this was the only story, but it was just the most recent. I could write an entire book on the actual issues people have had to deal with when working with people that should not be in the industry or even in business.

The Worst Thing That Can Happen

I don't like to talk negatively about others, but am doing it here for your protection and because I want you to really understand the problem with using a company that you should not be.

I want to tell you about the worst news you can here. Let me set up the situation.

You filed for divorce in the past and assumed your divorce case was completed. The company you worked with said your divorce was filed and so you never verified. A few years went by and you met someone and decided to get married. For some reason or another you need to get a copy of the divorce decree, say because the church wants to verify.

So you try to find your paperwork and can only find pieces or can't find it at all. You try to determine what your case number is so you can try to call the court to get a copy of your judgment. That's when it happens. That is when you realize your divorce was never finalized.

I am not kidding. I probably get two calls a month where someone calls to realize that their divorce was never finalized. Some found out because, like I said, they needed because they were getting married, or sometimes they find out because they are applying for a home loan or something where an entity would need a copy of the divorce decree.

But the worst is where someone has already been remarried. You heard me right. They have already been remarried. Many of them have entirely new families and new kids and have been remarried for numerous years. Imagine you find out this news. These folks are crying on the phone and can't believe that their divorce was never finalized. They ask me how they could possibly tell their spouse.

As a personal note, if you find yourself in this position is does not mean your current marriage is void. I have recorded several videos and podcasts on this issue. There is a lot of bad information out there that says your marriage is void. It is not true so you can relax.

Enough on this issue. I think you get the point that you need to use a Legal Document Assistant only. And if you live in California you need to be using my service as we serve all of California. You can learn more at www.divorce661.com.

Changing The Perception Of The LDA Industry

I don't like the perception that people have about Legal Document Assistants. I didn't like it when I started my business and I don't like it today. While I do everything in my power to change how people view what we do, I am in the minority.

Several years ago before I got into this business I did a ton of research. I looked at who was operating in my local area, what other LDA's were doing and how they were marketing themselves. I did not like what I saw. I saw LDA's marketing themselves as an low-end services. Don't get me wrong, that is a powerful message, but they were marketing themselves to people of very little means. They were marketing themselves to people who were very low income. They were giving the appearance that the only people of limited means work with Legal Document Assistants. Before you think I am jerk, let me explain. This did not make sense to me because the self-help centers at the courts are there to provide these services.

Here is the current mold of an LDA business. Set up shop in a high traffic area near a court house with good drive by traffic. Hang your business sign offering paralegal services and hope people walk in. You know what I am talking about. You drive by an unsightly corner shopping center. The kind of shopping center you would expect to find a laundromat in. You get what I am saying, right? You see that the windows are painted with glass paint that says, "divorce $299". I seriously cringe when I see these signs and feel this is to blame why people have a poor opinion of what we do or ask me if we can handle "their type of case."

I do a lot of marketing, both in a written format on my blog, but also in video format on my Youtube channel and on my audio podcast where you can find our podcast listed under, "Divorce Master Radio" on iTunes. Let me give you an example of the misperception of the Legal Document Assistant industry. I recently met a divorce mediator who had reached out to me and I invited him onto the radio show. I like to do interviews of people in my industry so I can provide additional resources to people going through divorce. We did the interview and all was well. Then after the interview we got to talking. At one point in the conversation he says, "my guess is that you work with people who earn under $50,000 combined household income."

I was shocked. Even people in the same business space have the opinion that Legal Document Assistants work with lesser earning income folks. I am not bashing people that make $50,000 mind you, he was referring to a combined household income of $50,000 so $25,000 per person. That is $1,000 per month. So, of course, I informed him of who our client base truly is. I also told him about the types of divorce cases we handle as well, because he also thought we handled very simple divorce cases.

So here is the deal. The clients that we work with, if I had to take an average the 1000's of clients I have worked with, I would say that the average household income is approximately $125,000. Most of our clients make at least $50,000 each and many make over $75,000 each. In addition to that, we have many clients where each spouse earns over $100,000 each. Of course we do have some that make less and some that make more, but this is the segment of the business that makes up the bulk of my business.

But there is a reason for that. It is how I do my marketing. I am not marketing to the people who would qualify for self help through the courts and asking them to "step up" to our service. No, I am marketing to the folks that would normally call attorneys and don't know that a better option exists. They are actually "stepping down" in costs from using an attorney when they decide to use us.

I did not understand at first why divorce attorneys did not like me. My impression is that I was helping people that did not need attorneys for the most part and I was not taking away any of their business.. But my business was not well received in our community or throughout California. It seems the divorce attorney community was okay with the people operating here for years because they did not know how to market themselves and were not on anybody's radar. However, I am constantly harassed by divorce attorneys either complaining to our local BAR association or by them writing articles in our local publication and speaking negatively towards my industry and my business specifically.

But here is the deal and how I feel about it. If people are using my service for their divorce, they never needed a divorce attorney in the first place and I think the attorneys know that. I also think that attorneys were taking on divorce cases that even they knew did not need an attorney to represent them, but they took the case because they needed the money and knew that their client hiring them had no idea there was another, better service to serve them.

Types Of Divorce Cases Legal Document Assistants Handle

Not all Legal Document Assistants are created equal. I must state that up front. Just because you hire an legal Document Assistant, does not mean anything. You still need to do your due diligence and make sure they are qualified.

My office handles 30+ divorce cases per month, more than any other Legal Document Assistant company in California. This is because we only specialize in divorce and all family law related matters. Most other LDA's do 20+ different services just to get by. How can you become an expert at anything when you spread your services across so many different fields. In fact, remember when I told you I had done my research prior to starting this business? I had noticed that everyone doing this was handling multiple areas of law and not just a single area like divorce.

But divorce was all I knew. And I was concerned that my business would not be successful because I was only efficient in one area of law. But this worry was misplaced. As it turns out, by specializing in a single area of law, that being family law and divorce, more people wanted to work with me, not only because they were aware of my background, but because all we handled was divorce day in and day out and became the go-to company in California.

Now to the topic of this section. What types of divorce cases do we handle? Again, another misunderstood issue that I want to dispel. This is what I get asked from people calling about getting help with their divorce. They will say something like, "I have a house and a pension... are you able to handle a divorce like this?" or, "I have children and we have a home and two rental properties, is this something divorce661.com can handle?"

This goes back to the perception people have of this industry, so I get where the question is coming from. But you probably know by now that the answer is Yes, we can help you. I have handled divorce cases with multiple properties, rental properties, multiple pensions, 401k's, deferred comp plans, spousal support orders, child support orders, people with businesses and even multiple businesses. I have helped people who are Law Enforcement, Fireman, Business owners, Doctors, other attorneys and folks who have intellectual property, etc., etc. I won't bore you, but we can handle any level of complexity.

Do you want to know what the common denominator is regarding the type of divorce cases we can handle are? It comes down to whether or not the spouses are willing to at least attempt to cooperate and work collaboratively to try and get through the divorce process. It does not matter the amount of assets you have, it has to do with the level of commitment the spouses have at working towards an agreement.

Even then, as I previously stated, we are able to handle divorce cases where the parties will certainly need an attorney, or even need mediation which I discuss in the next chapter, but want to save money at the outset of the divorce process so they can have better use of their money when they actually need an attorney.

Legal Document Assistants Serve The Middle Market

Okay, listen, you have the self help centers that provide free services to folks who qualify based upon income. Let's say they serve the bottom 20% of income earners. They are receiving free legal services. They can't afford attorneys or even the professional assistance of a Legal Document Assistant. So there is a program for them. Then, on the other end of the spectrum, you have the top 20% of income earners. These folks can probably afford an attorney for their divorce. But here is what I have said for years on my podcast, blog and on video. "Where do the people who fall in the middle turn to?"

For people who either can't afford to hire an attorney or who are smart enough to know that they don't want to spend the money on an attorney, even If they have it, where do they turn for help with their divorce? We are talking about a huge group by the way. By my estimation, we are talking about this middle 60% of the people who need our professional services, and that is why I am trying to get the word out to these folks that there is assistance they can obtain.

When I first got into this business, I noticed this was a very underserved market. On one hand you had people using attorneys for their divorce even though they didn't really need one, they just thought there was no other choice. Or you have the folks that don't want to hire an attorney because they don't want to spend the money and feel they have nowhere else to turn, and then try to do it themselves which never has a good outcome.

Whether or not my calculations are correct or not, the fact of the matter is that more divorce cases are handled without attorneys than with. That is why we handle 30+ divorce cases per month and an average attorney may have 1 or 2 new clients per month. We are able to conduct our business on volume vs. only getting one or two clients per month and trying to get as much money as we can out of them.

Chapter 7

DIVORCE MEDIATION

I could not write this book and not have a section dedicated to mediation. I want to take a page or two and explain to you the different types of divorce mediation services out there, because like with Legal Document Assistants, all are not created equal. I want to do this because mediation can play an important role during your divorce. Before you read this book, you may have thought that hiring an attorney was the only way to get through your divorce. I even asked my own wife the other day. I said, "what is the first word that comes to your mind after you hear the word divorce?" She said, "attorney." It is just how it is, but now you know there are options.

Many of our divorce clients are amicable and don't need any other third party services such as mediation or an attorney. But sometimes we will have a clients that run into trouble and they are stuck on a few points of their divorce agreement. They are not fighting, rather they just need assistance with coming to an agreement.

Usually how this comes up is our clients will call and ask for a referral to an attorney. I will ask them why they need an attorney. They usually say that they are having difficulty figuring out a few things as part of their agreement. See, they are not in disagreement and don't have a contested case that would require an attorney, they just don't know that there is any other options. They don't need an attorney, they need a mediator. Why do I push mediation over attorneys? The answer is cost mostly, but because I just believe that if folks can work out an agreement between themselves, they will end up with a much better agreement.

Different Types Of Divorce Mediators

There are different types of divorce mediators out there and you need to be aware of this. The clients that use my divorce service have the benefit of being referred by me to a divorce mediator and don't have to try to figure it out on their own. What I generally do is see what types of problems they are having and make a decision on the type of mediator they may need or may best suit the issues they are having.

I put divorce mediators into the following buckets. First, you have attorney mediators and non-attorney mediators. Second, you have what I call professional, paid mediation and mediation that occurs in court. There is a much different type of mediation style among them. In addition, their isn't much of a standard to becoming a mediator. I could call myself a mediator today, and probably have better skills than most, what with my background as a police officer, but that is not what I have decided to do. I bring this up to say that there can be a big difference between a mediators training and the end product you receive. Let's get into the different types of mediators and you will be able to see the difference.

Attorney Mediators

Let's start with the attorney mediators. Attorney mediators were not to prevalent in the years past, but now just about every divorce attorney offers some form of mediation. This is because they were losing money to people who were choosing non-attorney mediators so they figured they better offer mediation as well. But you get a much different mediation style from a divorce attorney who also says the do mediation.

It all comes down to mindset of the mediator. Attorney mediators are litigators first and mediators second. They went to law school and their main focus as a divorce attorney is to protect their clients and provide legal advice and get them the "best deal" they can in their divorce. When you have this type of mindset, it is hard for the attorney to make distinctions when providing mediation.

In mediation they need to play a neutral role, but their mindset is litigation. In my personal opinion, If you are going to use an attorney mediator, it would be best to use a non litigating divorce attorney. Meaning use a divorce attorney that only does mediation and does not handle court cases or represent clients. There is one advantage to using an attorney mediator and that is that they can provide legal advice so you can make informed decisions about the agreements you want to make in your divorce. However, knowing the law is only one part and isn't always necessary.

In fact, I believe true mediation is about what you feel is fair and working with your spouse towards an agreement that is mutually acceptable by both parties. When you conclude divorce mediation with an attorney, you will usually end up with what is known as a Marital Settlement Agreement which documents your agreements and can be used to file with the court. Okay, that covers attorney mediators, let's move on to non-attorney mediators.

Non-Attorney Mediators

This section covers what I call non-attorney mediators, also known as professional mediation. When I say professional mediation, I am talking about the mediator sitting in the room with both spouses and helping guide the conversation. Non-attorney mediators can run the gamut of experience. There are all types of training they could have taken, or not, and there different results you can receive from your mediation. I have interviewed numerous different mediators over the years and they all take a little different approach to their meditation style.

As I mentioned earlier, if you happen to be one of our clients, I will try to give you some guidance and set you up with the mediator who I think would be the best fit based upon the circumstances, other than that I do have some advice for choosing your mediator which I will discuss later.

Non-attorney mediators are exactly that. They are not attorneys. So you may be wondering how a non-attorney can be a successful mediator. As I eluded to before, the focus on non-attorney mediation is based upon what is fair rather than what is the law. They are not going to be there to tell you, "what a judge would say" or give you legal advice. That is the beauty of what I consider to be true mediation. Sure, you may need to obtain some legal advice at some point during mediation or even afterwards. Who says you can't have your non-attorney divorce mediation reviewed by a divorce attorney? But keep in mind that if you do, you will be getting a totally different perspective. It will be from one of the law, vs. one you thought was a fair agreement. I say this so you can better see the difference in types of mediation available.

If you haven't figured it out, I am more pro non-attorney mediator. I just think there are so many advantages. It really goes back to the chapter where we discussed compromise. This style of mediation allows you to focus on working towards an agreement that is in the best interest of both parties.

Court Mediation

I think that when people hear the word, "mediation" that they are thinking this is something that is done by the court. While the court's do offer some level of mediation, it is generally limited. There is a huge difference between professional mediation and court mediation. Court mediation is generally provided when the spouses make the requests. One party can ask for mediation through the courts but that does not compel the other party to show up.

The best way I can show you the difference is by an example. Let's say that you both decided that you need help coming to your agreements. If you choose to do this through the court mediation services, generally you will have to have filed some type of court action. Sometimes you don't, It really depends on the individual court. When you use court mediation, they are basically there to document the agreements you already have, and not sit there for several hours trying to help you come to an agreement. That is not their job.

However, with professional mediation this is different. You are paying for their service and they will spend as much time as necessary to help you work through your decisions until you have everything resolved.

Speciality Mediators

Most mediators are more of generalist mediators, meaning they are equipped to handle the regular and normal issues that will come up during mediation such as custody, property division, etc. However, as mediation becomes more and more popular, mediators have been taking on different specialities. For instance, I met a mediator last month whose speciality was as a Certified Divorce Financial Analyst.

I had not met a mediator who distinguished himself in this

way and I was glad to meet him and now we are referring business to each other. Many of our clients, if they need mediation, it is in the area of dividing up their finances. Other specialties include those that say they specialize in child custody issues. If you feel that the help you need is in a specific area, it may be worth your while to see if you can find a mediator that handles your specific issues, but my guess Is that unless is it is of a super complex nature, you won't need a specialist. Just make sure the mediator you choose is able to handle the issues at hand.

How To Choose A Mediator

The best way to choose a mediator is to use your judgment. Interview a few and find one that not only meets your needs but who you get along with and feel would be a good neutral third party to assist you and your spouse. Keep in mind that the mediator may be there in a room with you for several hours over the course of your mediation so you won't want someone that you don't click with or that for some reason pushes your buttons. Of course, this would be best applied to both spouses.

Most mediators I know offer free initial phone consultations so they can get a feel as to what your needs are. Following that they will generally want to get the two of you in for a consultation so they can speak to both of you either in person or over the phone. This way the mediator can meet both spouses and make a determination based upon the needs and the attitudes of the spouses if mediation, at least with them, would be the way to go. You could sort of call it a mutual consultation. They want to see if you would be good fit for them and you want to see if they would be a good fit for you.

Cost of Mediation

The cost of mediation varies but I will tell you it will be less than hiring an attorney. Mediators all have different fees, but I can talk to you about what you can expect from my experience in working with them. While it's not a hard and fast rule, you can expect to pay more per hour for mediation as the experience of the mediator goes up. Again, this isn't always the case, because I know very good mediators that charge $200 per hour. (Yes, that is on the low end)

It also depends on what type of mediation you need. For instance, do you just have trouble having a conversation with your spouse? Is it hard just being in a room and if you could only have a conversation without arguing you would make some progress? In these cases It may just be a matter of having a mediator who is helpful in controlling the conversation so that it stays on track.

But what if your issues are a little more heated? Maybe you need something called co-mediation. This is where you have two mediators in a room. This, of course, would be more costly, but still less than separately having attorneys.

The type of mediator you choose and how much it costs will vary from one meditator to the next. That is why I just say use your gut. If it doesn't work out, you can always try another mediator. The cost benefit of using a mediator, regardless of the cost, is that you are paying one person and not two as in the case of each of you having attorneys. The time spent mediating your case will be much less as you are both there to make the decisions as you proceed.

Using Legal Document Assistant And Mediator To Complete Your Divorce

Most divorce mediators only handle the mediation side of the divorce. This means that they do not handle the court interface or court documents to help you file for divorce. The mediators I have spoken with like to do the mediation and then move on to the next case. We work with many divorce mediators throughout California to prepare the actual court documents either before, during or after the mediation had started. If you have not filed your divorce case yet, we can certainly help you. And if you need help finding a mediator in California or a suggestion or referral, just give me a call. Let me know you learned about us from this book and I would be happy to give you a referral to a divorce mediator in your area.

If you are a divorce mediator in California and are reading this book and looking for a professional Legal Document Assistant that you can trust to refer your clients to, we would welcome the conversation and opportunity. The biggest complaint we have had from divorce mediators when they call us for help is that they cannot find a company professional enough that they can refer in confidence. The divorce mediators we work with know that we will be a good extension of their business which provides additional value for their mediation firm. We can do the same for you.

Chapter 8

A BETTER WAY TO DIVORCE

I have an opinion on how people should start their divorce no matter what is going on. Yes, it is a little self serving, but nonetheless I believe it is the best way to go. Not only will it save you money, it may keep your divorce from spiraling out of control when it doesn't have to.

I have to refer back to my past career as a Police Officer with the Los Angeles Police Department as it makes more sense to explain this way. When I was a Police Officer and dealing with the public, we would, on occasion, come in contact with someone who did not want to cooperate. This meant that it may result in what is called a "use of force".

A use of force is just about anytime we put our hands on someone to control their behavior in any way for the most part. The type and level of force that would be used would escalate from just giving verbal commands to follow our orders and could escalate to having to use lethal force. There are several levels in between, but we would not start at lethal force and then work our way down to verbal commands. You get the point. The other policy was, "use the minimal force necessary to control the subject."

Using this analogy, you would want to start your divorce with the lowest level of force. This means you wouldn't just go right to hiring an attorney. That is like going to lethal force when it may not be necessary. You would want to try and work through the levels of force as used in the analogy. So it would look like this. You want to file for divorce. It may be amicable or it may not be. Just because it is not amicable does not mean you have to go out and hire an attorney. Not only is there a chance that you could resolve this yourself, you won't have to spend the money to hire an attorney and you may end up having a better post-divorce relationship.

This lowest level of force, in this case, would be using a Legal Document Assistant for the purposes of filing your divorce. Not only is this cost efficient, but you have the opportunity to tell your spouse, even if not amicable, that you would prefer not to have the expense of hiring attorneys for your divorce. Your spouse would see that you are taking a less forceful approach which would possibly keep the divorce from escalating. I can tell you from experience, that if you hire an attorney as your first action, the reaction is for your spouse to do the same. This is what we are trying to avoid.

As you move through the process of getting a divorce, let's say that you need some additional assistance with your divorce. Perhaps you have agreed to try and get through this without attorneys but you just need some help with the decisions. Great! In this case we are talking about mediation. Can you see how we by walking through the different tools in the arsenal for getting through your divorce you are using the correct tool as you need it?

So at this point you have hired the Legal Document Assistant to start the case. Non-threatening, right? You realize that you need a little more help and moved up the next level and try the mediation route. You will either be successful in mediation or you won't be. But I will tell you that mediation is very successful, but does depend in large part on the spouses involved. But let's say that after going this route, you just can't come to an agreement. Maybe there is just to much resentment or whatever else is going on and you decide to hire an attorney.

Even if this happens, which I hope it does not, several things have occurred. First, you saved a ton of money up to this point. Second, you probably resolved 90% of your issues so far. If you do end up having to hire an attorney, it is not going to be starting back at square one. It will just be a matter of your attorneys litigating the issues remaining. What this means is that you were not able to come to an agreement on your own and the attorneys are going to make the argument for you in front of a judge so the judge can make the decision for you.

Worst case scenario is that you used a Legal Document Assistant to start the case and do all the paperwork. You had a divorce mediator resolved 90% of your issues. The attorney only has to get you the other 10% of the way there. You would have saved so much money and heartache up to this point that it is well worth it.

Chapter 9

LIFE ON THE OTHER SIDE

I have handled a lot of divorce cases and helped a lot of spouses, whether it was in person or over the phone with their divorce. I wanted to share with you what I have seen and what I have been told by my clients once their divorce case if finally over. That there is life on the other side.

I have handled divorce cases where people have been married less than a week up to as long as being married for 55 years before filing for divorce. I know first-hand that time will handle any sorrows. How much time is the unknown factor.

But I have to be honest with you. The majority of my clients are happy when their divorce is completed, like visibly happy almost immediately. It may have something to do with the fact that we are not handling high-conflict divorce cases, or it may be because they were living in a situation for so long that they didn't want to be in, but for whatever reason continued to stick it out. Whatever it is, our clients call and email us when they get their final divorce papers in the mail from the court. They almost seem like different people.

Some clients report to us that once the divorce was over that they actually became friends with their ex-spouse and go out do dinner together with their kids on occasion. They say that whatever attachment being married had over them, that the minute they were divorced and no longer attached that the stress and anxiety that "being married" had on them just fell away.

I had a client come in this week with a copy of the final divorce papers that showed his divorce would be final in a month. He couldn't believe it and wanted to verify in person with me and then said when that date comes that we are going out for drink.

I could go on and on, but don't want to make it sound like divorce is a celebration or joyous occasion. I just want to get across that in my experience, with the kind of cases we handle and how we handle them that people come out okay on the other side. And I hope you will too.

Chapter 10

FINAL THOUGHTS

There were many reasons for this book. While we covered several topics, the main goal was to help show people that there is a better way to get divorced and that there are better options for divorce that you may have not been aware of . This book was just one more format to help educate you about divorce and your options. To encourage you to take steps that you may not have otherwise done on your own.

I am truly passionate about helping people avoid the pitfalls when considering divorce. To help save you money and guide you in a better direction so you, your spouse and children are in the best condition post divorce as you can be. I offered some sound advice and hope you decide to act on it. I hope that you are not one of those people that are being dragged through the mud and have one of those horrible divorce cases that we seem to always hear about.

I am aware that you took a leap of faith when you purchased this book and for that I want to personally thank you for reading it. While I feel there was great value even if you read just one chapter, I know that to read the entire book provides much better insight to the point I was trying to get across.

Chapter 11

BONUS CHAPTER & FREE STUFF

I wanted this book to be worth it's while. While I know you got something out of this book, I wanted to provide more than what I could put in it. I had mentioned before that I had an online do-it-yourself divorce service as well as my full-service divorce program.

I personally created the online do-it-yourself divorce service and it is chock full of additional information, including video interviews of mediators, interviews of realtors where we talk real estate and divorce, interviews with insurance agents where we talk insurance and divorce and much, much more. We usually charge $97 for access to this resource at

www.CaliforniaDivorceTutor.com but for the readers of this book, this information is free. For access all you need to do is send me an email to Tim@divorce661.com and in the subject line write, "Why You Don't Need A Divorce Attorney Book" and ask for access.

Thank you again, I am humbled that you got to know a little about me.

www.ingramcontent.com/pod-product-compliance
Lightning Source LLC
Chambersburg PA
CBHW060413190526
45169CB00002B/876